My cousin and I look alike. My aunt and uncle say we look like siblings. My mommy and daddy say we look like siblings. My grandma and grandpa, the whole family, even our friends, say we look like siblings. More like twin sisters actually, like our mothers did when they were children.

我表妹和我长得很像。我的阿姨和姨父说，我们看起来就像亲姐妹。我的爸爸妈妈说，我们看起来就像亲姐妹。我的外婆外公，全家所有人，甚至我们的朋友，都说我们像亲姐妹。其实我们更像双胞胎，就像我们的母亲小时候那样。

When we were little, we lived next door to each other. To see her, all I had to do was cross the tall grass in front of our house, open the gate and enter her garden. We met every day and played all sorts of games. She was my neighbor and best friend. But then she moved.

小的时候，我们住在隔壁。为了见到她，我要做的就是穿过家门口高高的草地，打开大门，钻进她的花园。我们每天都见面，玩各种各样的游戏。她是我的邻居，也是我最好的朋友。但是，后来她搬家了。

Now she lives in a faraway land, and I miss her so much. Mommy said to try and find something positive no matter the circumstances. There's always something to be grateful for. And so I did. My cousin and I are very lucky. Despite the distance between us, we can still talk, play, and see each other often via video chat. We talk about everything!

现在，她住在一个很远很远的地方，我非常想她。妈妈说，不管在什么环境下，都要努力找到积极的一面。总有一些事情是值得感激的。于是，我照做了。我和表妹都很幸运。尽管我们之间的距离很远，但我们仍然可以经常通过视频聊天来交谈、玩耍和见面。我们无话不谈！

The last time we met online, she told me that it's winter and very cold there. Everything is covered in snow. She snowboards, skis, and goes ice skating with her new friends.

上一次我们在网上见面的时候，她告诉我，她那里是冬天，非常冷。一切都被雪覆盖着。她和她的新朋友们去滑单板，滑双板，还有滑冰。

I told her that it's summer
and very hot here.

我告诉她，我这儿是夏天，非常
热。

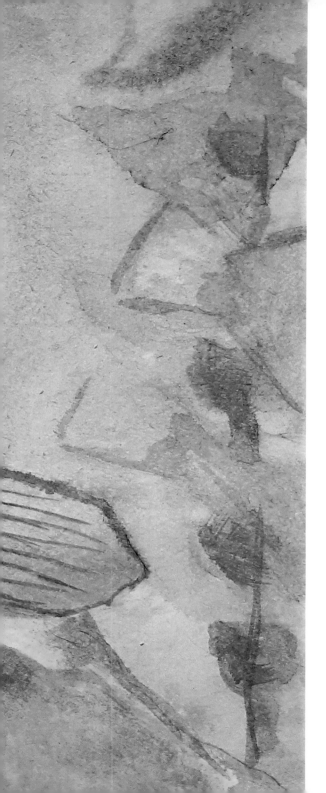

I swim and snorkel every day with our old friends, and we watch the most beautiful fish underwater.

我和我们的老朋友每天都去游泳和浮潜，在水下观看最美丽的鱼。

Then, we spoke about animals.
She said mammals with fur white
as snow live in the
northern part of her country:
polar bears, arctic foxes, seals.

然后，我们聊起了动物。她说，在
她那个国家的北部，生活着皮毛洁
白如雪的哺乳动物：北极熊、北极
狐、海豹。

I had hoped she would also talk about monkeys, but it turns out they don't live there at all!

我本来希望她会说起猴子，可是，原来它们根本就不住在那里！

She also asked about her pet which stayed behind with me. I answered that her cat is in very good hands and gets lots of cuddles and kisses.

她还问起了她留给我的宠物。我回答说，有人把她的猫照顾得很好，给它很多抱抱和亲亲。

And I still go to the park on Sundays,
and feed the ducks we both love
so much.

星期天我还是会去公园，喂那些我们
都很喜欢的鸭子。

Then, my cousin used some foreign words, and in an accent, I didn't recognize. I felt confused. She said she couldn't remember how to say "mountain", "rocks", and "river", and that she now talks more in her father's language.

然后，表妹说了一些外国词语，口音也不一样，我没有听懂。我觉得很困惑。她说她不记得"山"、"石"和"河"怎么说了，现在她更经常讲她父亲的语言。

She explained that sometimes it's hard for her to find the right words in our language. I told her I understand. I'm also learning another language at school, and it should be fun to compare words from our different languages.

她解释说，有时候她很难在我们的语言中找到合适的词。我告诉她，我明白。我也在学校学习另一种语言，我们用不同语言中的词语来做比较，应该会很有趣。

That is how we came up with the "Word Swap" painting game. My cousin painted a cactus, and then both of us said the word out loud. "Cactus" sounds similar in many of our languages!

我们就这样想出了"词语交换"的绘画游戏。表妹画了一株仙人掌，然后我们俩都大声说出了这个词。"仙人掌"在好几种语言里听起来都很像！

Her parents overheard us and joined the conversation. My aunt is a linguist and she told us that there are currently over 7,000 known spoken languages around the world! My uncle is a language teacher and he challenged us to swap a couple more words. We kept on going for a while with words like "flower", "water", "love", and "friendship".

她的父母无意中听到了我们的谈话，也加入进来。我的阿姨是一位语言学家，她告诉我们，目前世界上已知的口语就超过了7000种！我的姨父是一位语言老师，他让我们挑战一下，多交换几个词语。我们又继续说了"花"、"水"、"爱情"和"友谊"这些词。

Next time we video chat, I will share this painting I made for her. I would like to swap the word "home".

下次我们视频聊天的时候，我会分享我为她做的这幅画。我想和她交换的词是"家"。

Traditional Chinese

永遠的表姐妹

我表妹和我長得很像。我的阿姨和姨父說，我們看起來就像親姐妹。我的爸爸媽媽說，我們看起來就像親姐妹。我的外婆外公，全家所有人，甚至我們的朋友，都說我們像親姐妹。其實我們更像雙胞胎，就像我們的母親小時候那樣。

小的時候，我們住在隔壁。為了見到她，我要做的就是穿過家門口高高的草地，打開大門，鑽進她的花園。我們每天都見面，玩各種各樣的遊戲。她是我的鄰居，也是我最好的朋友。但是，後來她搬家了。

現在，她住在一個很遠很遠的地方，我非常想她。媽媽說，不管在甚麼環境下，都要努力找到積極的一面。總有一些事情是值得感激的。於是，我照做了。我和表妹都很幸運。儘管我們之間的距離很遠，但我們仍然可以經常通過視頻聊天來交談、玩耍和見面。我們無話不談！

上一次我們在網上見面的時候，她告訴我，她那裏是冬天，非常冷。一切都被雪覆蓋着。她和她的新朋友們去滑單板，滑雙板，還有滑冰。

我告訴她，我這兒是夏天，非常熱。

我和我們的老朋友每天都去游泳和浮潛，在水下觀看最美麗的魚。

然後，我們聊起了動物。她說，在她那個國家的北部，生活着皮毛潔白如雪的哺乳動物：北極熊、北極狐、海豹。

我本來希望她會說起猴子，可是，原來它們根本就不住在那裏！

她還問起了**她**留給我的寵物。我回答說，有人把**她**的貓照顧得很好，給**它**很多抱抱和親親。

星期天我還是會去公園，喂那些我們都很喜歡的鴨子。

然後，表妹說了一些外國詞語，口音也不一樣，我沒有聽懂。我覺得很困惑。**她**說**她**不記得"山"、"石"和"河"怎麼說了，現在**她**更經常講**她**父親的語言。**她**解釋說，有時候**她**很難在我們的語言中找到合適的詞。我告訴**她**，我明白。我也在學校學習另一種語言，我們用不同語言中的詞語來做比較，應該會很有趣。

我們就這樣想出了"詞語交換"的繪畫遊戲。表妹畫了一株仙人掌，然後我們倆都大聲說出了這個詞。"仙人掌"在好幾種語言裏聽起來都很像！

她的父母無意中聽到了我們的談話，也加入進來。我的阿姨是一位語言學家，她告訴我們，目前世界上已知的口語就超過了7000種！我的姨父是一位語言老師，他讓我們挑戰一下，多交換幾個詞語。我們又繼續說了"花"、"水"、"愛情"和"友誼"這些詞。

下次我們視頻聊天的時候，我會分享我為她做的這幅畫。我想和她交換的詞是"家"。

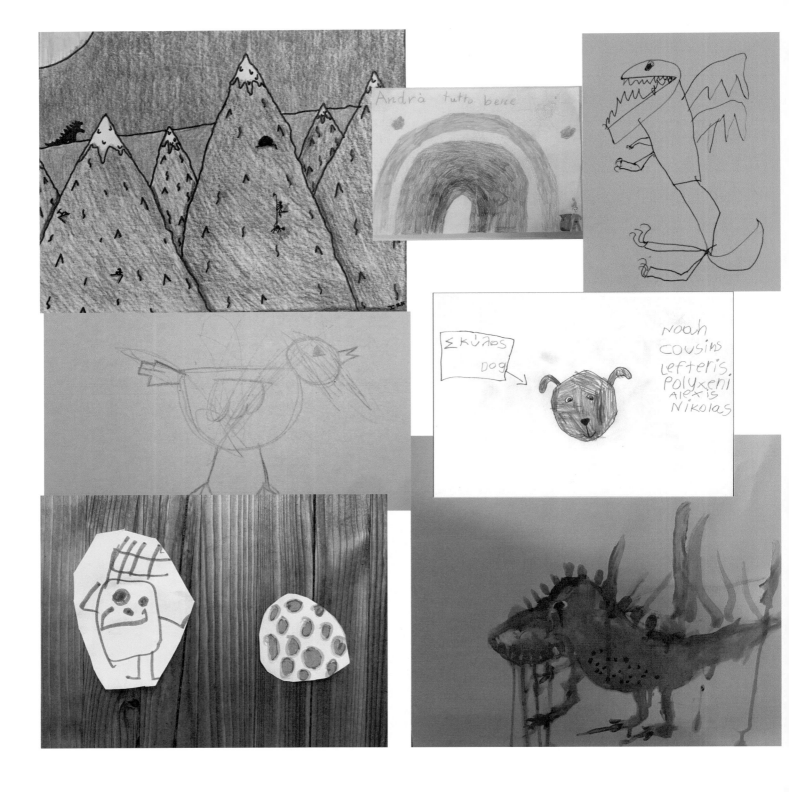

Unicorn - Ioli
Μονόκερος - Ιόλη

Ioli - Unicorn
Ιόλη - Μονόκερος

The Word Swap Game - Meet the children!

Erik, Nelly, Iason, Iria, Sadiq, Tariq, Vincent, Rukeiya, Lea, Hector, Victor, Orestis, Odysseas, Noah, Polyxeni, Lefteris, Alexis, Nikolas,Iahn, Chloe, Ioli, Rea, Nicolas, Sveva, Giuseppe, Zafiris, Dimitris, Periklis, Vaggelis, Andrea, Zaira, Philippos, Nefeli, Baby, George, Emmanuela, Mason, Ethan, Elijah, Oliver, Athina, Apolonas, Alexandros, John, Martina, Steffy, Thanos, Nikolai, Areti, Nikolai, Nina, Nicol, Joni, Mia, Emma, Stella, Artemis, Mirto, Antonis, Nicolas, Mihalis, Katerina, Nikos, Alexis, Liam, Olivia, Noah, William, Ava, Jacob, Isabella, Patricia, Hannah, Matthew, Ashley, Samantha, Maureen, Leanne, Kimberly, David, Marie, Vasilis, Yiannis, Kyra, Joakim, Alexander, Nikolas, Ellie, Sebastian, Sophie, Sabina, Stepan, Vasilis, Yiannis, Kyra, Youjin, Sejin, Okito, Magdalini, Nicoletta, Efimia, Didi, Bia, Timo, Vittoria.

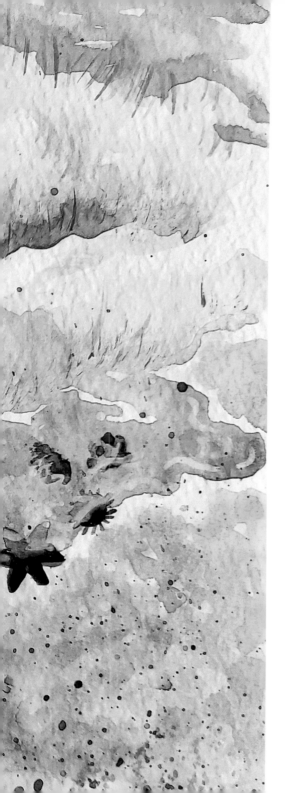

Dear Child,

I hope you enjoyed this story. If you'd also like to play the "Word Swap" game, ask an adult to help you, if needed, to write down your favorite word, and then draw or paint it. Your guardian can send me your painting via email at liza@maltamum.com, and I'll share it with other parents and children in my Facebook group "Elisavet Arkolaki's Behind The Book Club".

Dear Grown-up,

If you feel this book adds value to children's lives, please leave an honest review on Amazon or Goodreads. A shout-out on social media and a tag #CousinsForeverWordSwap would also be nothing short of amazing. Your review will help others discover the book, and encourage me to keep on writing. Visit eepurl.com/dvnij9 for free activities, printables and more.

Forever grateful, thank you!

All my best,
Elisavet Arkolaki

Made in United States
Troutdale, OR
04/18/2025

30695945R00024